GLURK!

A HELLBENDER ODYSSEY

MARK SPITZER

ANAPHORA LITERARY PRESS

AUGUSTA, GEORGIA

ANAPHORA LITERARY PRESS
2419 Southdale Drive
Hephzibah, GA 30815
http://anaphoraliterary.com

Book design by Anna Faktorovich, Ph.D.

Author's photo by Russ Hancock
Cover image © David Herasimtschuk, 2015

Published in 2016 by Anaphora Literary Press

Glurk! A Hellbender Odyssey
Mark Spitzer—1st edition.

ISBN-13: 978-1-68114-231-9
ISBN-10: 1-68114-231-7

Library of Congress Control Number: 2016900991

GLURK!

A HELLBENDER ODYSSEY

MARK SPITZER

The Electric Hellbender

CONTENTS

Acknowledgments

Poems I-V were published in *Cave Region Review*.

Poems I-V can also be found online at:
www.youtube.com/watch?v=lVHvBd9Lpxc.

CRYPTODUCTION

I n drafting this quixotically flamboyant epic hybrid focused on North America's most mongo salamander, I chose the enigmatic structural form of *Cryptobranchus alleganiensis*: a twisting species with all sorts of squiggle-rhythms wiggilating fluidly. Which is why the language here is both playful and extravagant—to mimic this amphibian.

Hence "the electric hellbender": a reassembled Stratocaster with whammy bar and distortion box built into a crypto-conglomeration of drainage tubing, insulating foam, and uncooked lasagna noodles that creates flubbery feedback undulations (see "Glurk1 Spitzer" on YouTube). Modeled on the mysterious hellbender, whose unique character remains elusive and abstract, I built this contraption to complement and embellish a strangely ornate body of investigative poetics, and to spread the Gospel of Glurk. The result being an admittedly audacious exploitation of poetic license complete with literal and auditory tangential frills.

What follows, therefore, is a narrative that relies on folklore, salamander scholarship, conservation efforts, and personal experience to send a semi-absurd yet solemn package of environmental messages. En route, the science cited comes from the communal corpus of bender biology, which is really real; even in Book III, which imagines and extrapolates a hellbender's point of view. As a rogue form of science fiction crossed with poetry and creative nonfiction, the intention with Book III was to reflect the plight of an evolutionary phenomenon that has as much to say about humans and our relationship with the natural world as it does about the hellish bender itself.

I'd like to thank Susan Gallagher, Director of Public Relations at the St. Louis Zoo, and Mark Wanner, Zoological Manager of Herpetology & Aquatics at the Zoo's WildCare Institute, for taking time to give me a tour of the Ron Goellner Center for Hellbender Conservation, where many of my hellbendish questions were answered and addressed. Thanks also to Kelly Irwin of the Arkansas Game and Fish Commission for letting me tag along on a hellbending expedition with US Fish & Wildlife. Gratitude as well for feedback and support from Dr. Donald Shepard, Amphibian

Authority at University of Louisiana at Monroe, and Dr. Anna Factorovitch of Anaphora Literary Press. Mucho appreciation to Sparky the Snot Otter as well. May all your toes regenerate!

—Mark Spitzer, 2015.

BOOK I

PROFILES IN HELLBENDAGE

I. GLURK, HELLBENDER!

Through the viscous crystalline of yr spring-fed Salamandria
through yr burbling bebouldered waterways
through eons of amphibious evolution
      dating back
      to the Jurassic

    Glurk Glurk
    w/ yr wide & comic muppet mouth
    & those flabby epidermal flaps
    filled with the stuff of oxy-suck
    because you breathe through micro-tubes
    hidden in yr webby skin
    skirting both
    nauga-sides

        Glurk Glurk
        w/ yr warty widdle toes
        awiggle in the jiggle stream
        which actually have
        grippy pads
        for traction on the algaed scree

        Glurk Glurk
        because that's what you do
        crawling crawling into the current
        sliding slimy under rocks

            w/ yr flat bodied
            dorsally ventricated
            low belly structure
            acting like a spoiler
            holding Glurks to Planet Earth
            aqua   dynamically

Glurk w/ yr oar shaped tail
    keeled primarily for propulsion!
    You freaky bizarro weirdo creature
    actually hearing
    through yr jaw!

    Glurk the largest
        wrinkliest
            under-glurker of yr class
                sometimes surpassing
                    two feet long

    Glurk you strangely ornate living salami
    you jerky liver sausage lizard
    trimmed with rippling
    riffles of roast beef

    glurking around all splotchy brown
        or orangish with a rusty tinge
            yr entire
                spotty
                    squiggle-skin
          slickened with photo
            sensitive
            cells

                    Glurk, Hellbender
                    glurk in lurk
                    of Oblivion!

II. HOW THE HELL-BENDER GLURKED ITS NAME

Theory #1
came straight from the settlers:

Glurking grotesque and grodily
    this bastardly mass cast out of hell
    is bent on bending
    its way back

       —undulating
        infernally!

But then there's Theory #2
according to Barton (1812)
in which "the negroes" of Virginia
saw "its slow twisted motions" as
the "tortuous pangs of the damned in hell"

       —undulating
        infernally!

III. SALAMANDRA HORRIDA LINGUISTICA

Glurk hellbender
Glurk snot otter |
Glurk devil-dog
water-dog
but Glurk not
mudpuppy
                    (cuz that's a whole
                    nuther species)

Glurk, however, mud-devil
ground puppy
Allegheny
alligator
                    (not to mention
                    just plain old "Alligator"
                    "young alligator"
                    or "little alligator")

    —or grampus
    —or volgo
    —or waterdog
    —or hogfish
    —or walking catfish
    —or big water lizard
    —or lasagna lizard
    —or any other glurking rose
        by any other
        glurking name

            like "Tweeg"
            like "Tweche"
                    (monikers monikered
                    by Delaware tribes)

or "Twechk"
                (Minsi)
or "To-ko-meg"
                (Chippewa)

another name that never stuck
was "Leverian Water-Newt"
so named by a Dr. Shaw
at the Leverian Museum
back in 1800s England

        a time when taxonomists
        were trying to classify
        every glurking thing on earth

        hence this mystery ichthyoid
        was lumped among "the doubtful reptiles"
        the entire hellbendy genus
        labeled *Gigantea*

        even the French got in on it
        when a Monsieur Michaux
        donated one to the Jardin des Plantes
        which Latreille later dubbed
        "Salamandre des monts Alléganis"
            which also failed to take

                same thing with *Menobranchus*
                        (meaning "minus gills")
                which evolved from a 19th-century combo
                of *Menopoma* and *Abranchus*
                        (these names also
                        never took)

as for the final Latin incarnation
because benders are born w/ fringy gills
which eventually shrink into gooey slits
spiracally set behind the neck
Cryptobranchus came along
meaning "hidden gills"

        because that's the absence
        of what these cryptic critters got
        glurking through
        the Underglurk!

IV. THE GLURKOGRAPHICS

Glurk Glurk two separate subspecies
the Eastern and Ozarkian
glurking threatened
throughout their range

though only the Ozark is endemic
        to Arkansas and Missouri
& is an officially listed
endangered species

while the Eastern glurks in sixteen states
from MO to NY
then down to Georgia
and back to Tennessee
w/ all that mountainous in-between
anemic of hellbendery

most populations have lead-zeppelined
seventy to eighty percent
in a third of a century

in fact   pretty much all colonies
have alarmingly few
juvies in the mix

        so glurk on that
        hellbenderer!

V. ADDERALL COLLATERAL

Glurk Glurk Glurk
flurbilating furiously
floobing out
falubriously

    glurking glurking gloobily
    globbily
    glibberating
    lugubriously

        flurkilating frillily
        flarkilating
        glurbily

           glarkelating
           Glurkensteins
           glurbilating
           galoobriously

glooop...   *glooop...*   *glooop...*
    glop...   *glop...*   *glog....*

    —all hellbenders are going down
        that's the prognosis

    —the whole damned species
        scheduled as a sacrifice
        for our freedom
        to expand

    Glurk That!

    Glurk
    this.

VI. HELLBENDERS: WHAT ARE THEY GOOD FOR?

in the literature of Benderosity
not much is known
about human consumption

but Swanson, Beck and Minton mention   (1948) (1965) (1972)
salacious salamandage
& Brimley says they're "good eating"   (1939)

according to Lang   (1968)
woodland natives ate 'em up
whereas Barton points to other tribes   (1812)
drying hides
for "purposes of witchcraft"

Nickerson and Mays   (1972)
   note another unique utility
seems a Pennsylvania resident
once put one in his booze-cooling pond
to scare away his mother-in-law
   supposedly
"it worked!"

VII. 2014 OZARK HELLBENDER FEST
POCAHONTAS, AR

we camped in the old settlement park
then drove into town
saw the famous asteroid
and made our way
to the square

the first place we stopped
was a run down junk shop
that used to be the local brothel
they had plow parts, jars of jam
and an antique cathode ray machine

but they also had one remaining
"SAVE THE HELLBENDER" t-shirt
made in Spain
which I bought

Armadillo Jeff was pumped to run
the annual Hellbender 5K
but there was no registration tent

also
the hellbender lecture had been canceled
because of the recent F4
that wiped out the Game & Fish Commish
down in Central Arkansas

& there was no Hellbender Auction this year
& there was no Hellbender Boogie Dice Biker Run
but across from the old court house
there was a dumpy lumpy
sculpture of one

so we saw the quilts
we bypassed the clogs
and went to the Randolph County
Historical Museum

to see the jumbo gator gar
it was seven feet long w/ yellowed fins
from being displayed for sixty years

which made this trip
almost worth it.

VIII. GLURKING NOCTURNAL, SLURPING WORMS

Glurking larvae, glurking bugs
     minnows, frogs, polliwogs
Glurking toads, glurking snakes
     snails, clams, hellgrammites
even smaller salamanders
     plus the putricene
     of deadflesh

     but most of all
     glurking crayfish
     aka ninety percent
     of El Glurko's
     hell-diet
          (though lampreys have been found in esophagi
             along with "un-
               identified mammals")

     meanwhile
     hellbenders hunt
          snuffling grub
ranging thirty to sixty feet from slab-abode
where glurksters glurk for thirty years
and fifty in captivity
               rarely roaming more than a mile

     glurking their glurking
          tastebuds off
     stalking scents
          gauging vibrations
     through hypersensitive
          lateral lines

glurking because
     those lidless little
laboring eyes
     can hardly focus
on a single
     glurking thing

glurking because
their eyesight
sucks

glurking because
glurkity
glurk.

IX. GOLIATHS @ GOLGOTHA

Glurkity Glurk
in the dying of the light
you funny funky puppets of dearth
scouring the pebblitude

Glurkity Glurk
you last remaining
Giant American Salamander
cut off from yr ancient
Asian cousins:

the Chinese and Japanese Gigantomanders
glurking up to two meters long
two hundred years
& weighing well over
one hundred pounds

Glurkity Glurk
their dazed & desperate fuddlement
as seen on YouTube videos
emerging from urban drainage veins
stunned by the sun & searching for
the gone sparkle
of their source

these slimed and leprous phibians
frequently freak
good citizens out

baby strollers veer for cover
infants are whisked away
from a possible new
god-awful zilla-pox
portending
planetary
pocalypse

of creatures borne
into an ether-world
warming
warming
globally.

X. IT'S NOT EASY BEING A CRYPTOBRANCHOID

glurking on, the full grown hellbender
  is committed to his mission
    of staking out a rock for himself
      rarely glurking
        gregariously
          always glurking
          warily

        of serpentine death-slith
       turtle-snap
         rogue raccoonage
           otterness & minkitude

          such predators prey
             on the elder benders of the flow
               while mass juvies are slaughterized
               by even more fish 'n fowl

Here come the Bass! Here come the Trout!
Here come the Herons and the Hawks!
    But even worse
  here come the descendants
    of *Homo erectus*!

    The giggers and the fishermen!
      The farmers and construction trucks!
     Canoers and tubers turning rocks!
      Even trained researchers
        sticking and stabbing &
         plucking em out!

along with a maggot-slough of abductors
exploiting "exotics"
for blind profit

O my Opia
an entire genepool
swirling down the toilet
while we just stand there
staring bare bum
waiting for the final
irreversible
gurgling
"glurk!"

XI. HELLBENDER RAPRODUCTION

Glurk Hellbender
Glurk unto the Multitudes!
Glurk for five to seven years
till sexually mature

Glurk the horny hell-males
slurking the nights of early fall
sporting angry swollen rings
spanning glands and
cloaking cloaca

> to glurk a broodsite under log
> or glurk a depression under rock
> where they glurking wait
> like stalkers for a catamite

> > eventually
> > a gravid slimer sidles by
> > so nubile in newtitude
> > that he steers the glurkess
> > into his burrow

> > > where he holds her down
> > > and dryhumps her *moistiness*
> > > pressing and prodding and
> > > rubbing as he rocks
> > > until she finally

> > > OVIPOSITS!

ribbons of glorious
glutinous goo

the hostager then milts a spray
on two to seven
hundred eggs

fertilization is mucho efficient
thanks to "polyspermy" dynamics

aggressive zoas going gonzo
penetrating solo ova
maybe even
ten sperm per   (see Bertrand Smith, 1926)

by this time, howev
the ravager has tossed her out

so he can stay and guard that sauce
perhaps topping 2K eggs
from serial seizures
of under-rubble
hell-booty

but like bad dad cannibals
pa benders are prone to grubbing out
on their own jellied selves
& sometimes the mothers
do too

basic Benderology believes
such behavior is pop
ulation control.

XII. GENESIS AB UTERO

Glurk Hellbender!
Incubate in dark of den
undulate w/ aerating folds
rocking on haunches for forty five days
sixty five days
maybe even eighty days
then behold the birth
of hellions

the larvae are an inch long
with yolky sacs to snack upon
they have no
          functional limbs

but they do have
fancy flaring
lionesque gills
maning out
Leo
ly.

XIII. THE NUTMEAT OF THE MATTER

Glurk Glurkbenders!
Glurk as populations drop
      mostly from siltation
      and the cockblocking of
          migration routes

because benders are always on the decline
and dams are always damning them
along w/ Pollutio

      and, of course, Development
      cuz there's a direct correlation
      between forests &
      habitat:

      basically
      trees protect from Erosia
      & work to prevent
      sedimentation

Aye, Hellbender
aglurk w/in the cleanest streams
glurking for Water Quality

      for hellbenders are
      the measurement of
      a system's overall health

their ruffles sponge up particles
      pesticides
      heavy metals
      synthetic hormones
      whatever's out there
      swilling around

benders, therefore
      are slippery barometers
      of what all life in their sectors
      toxically consumes

      infactamundo:
      studies have shown
      declining baby gravy counts
      in environs of hell-decline

                               (*Wash Post*, Dec 5, 2011)

and don't forget
      most of us live downstream
      of the hellacious ones
      so if their numbers are going down
      there must be something
      in the water

      something
        coming
      our way.

XIV. INSULT TO INJURY

Glurking further
Glurking free (?)
Glurking in the
degradation

the habitat loss
the mining turbidity
the ag and urb
runoff of indulgences

plus timber harvest
nitrate overload
and impoundments constructed
for hydro-elec

hence:
loss of genetic diversity
reduced recruitment
and the increased threat
of climate change
now striking w/ synergy!

but that's just for starters
since we also have
canoe-conk
cattle plop
road rut
& predation by
stocked trout
& invasives

Lordy, Lordy
what's a poor
hellbender to do?

XV. A PLAGUE OF NECROTIC MURTILATION

Exacerbating all the above
we've also got a dreaded pox

—otherwise known
    as chytrid fungus
        an infectious disease
            laying waste to populations
            w/ no effective control

        this toxic pox has already afflicted
            thirty percent
            of worldwide amphibians

                                        (amphibianrescue.org)

            the pandemic started in California
                when infected African clawed frogs
                    injected with the urine of pregnant women
                    were released in the seventies

                        (see "Prevalence of *Batrachochytrium...*"
                                by Sherril Green *et alia*)

                    verdict being:
                        this stuff's been found
                            present in almost
                                all Ozark populations:

as eco-author Richard Conniff
    noted in May of 2013:
        "When spores of this fungus penetrate a victim's skin . . .
            dead cells builds up on the surface,
                blocking respiration. The electrolytes go out
                of balance. The brain swells."

and as other sources add
zoospores rage
while aquaborne pathogens
flash flagella
for locomotion

insisting on encysting
digits dissolving
feet corroding
exposing bone

then blindness, missing eyes
forked limbs, tumor-skin
even anorexia

and yea, convulsions
as ulcers ulce
& hemorrhages hem

then comes lethargy
glomming along
on the bottom

     in other words
     chy-fungus ain't
     just a bummer;
     it's a phibian
      eviscerating
     scourge.

BOOK II

RESEARCH & OUTREACHIO

XVI. ALL HAIL THE RON GOELLNER CENTER FOR HELLBENDER CONSERVATION

at the St. Louis Zoo
WildCare Institute
where deep in Herpetarium
a decade of Glurkiolgy
has led to an amphi-
Revolution

    this state of the art
    Ozark Hellbender Headquarters
    (a "flagship species" of the zoo)
    is the only place on the planet
    where these squeegee-skinned
    baby branchoids
    have been bred in captivity

        it took years of finding
        the balance betwixt
        hard and soft water
        replicating conditions in nature
        harvesting eggs from the field
        experimenting w/ hellbender huts
        & triggering Conceptio

    a thousand were raised in 2014
    and they're aiming for the same
    in '015

mission is
to find the decline
in order to preserve
various crashing crypto-clans

to the point that there are now
way more benders of Ozark hell
in this facility
        (which is dedicated exclusively
        to reintro and repop)
than actually exist
in das Wild.

XVII. INTO THE BELLY OF THE BEAST

Zoological Manager Mark Wanner
gave me a tour
starting with the Hall of Quarantine

> where feeder fish chill for three weeks
> in pretreated aquariums
> and ghost shrimps go
> thru an anti ick
> sodium dip
>
> contamination is no joke
> we even clean our soles
> in a scrub tub of chemicals
> before passing through
> the glurkin' gates

to the main chamber
where three full-time staffers
are supported by interns and volunteers
feeding and adjusting
watching where the water's at

> there are tons of tanks lining all walls
> jam-packed w/ all sizes
> of both Eastern and Ozarkians
> > though the Ozarks are more colorful
>
> but whatever sub
> species they are
> the young-of-year clump up
> jet-black and smooth of skin
> glumming from PVC pipes
> tubes and bubblers everywhere

they're tagged with chips
and flagged for infection
only those free of disease
are released at five
or six inches long

        in 2013
        seven hundred and six
        zoo-reared juvies
        were freed in native habitats
        w/ consistent figures
        following that

    meanwhile
    cuddly cuties grub in a pack
    chowing down like a bunch of pups
    gobbling for liberty.

XVIII. REWILDING IN ABSENTIA

hoofing on
we arrive at the first
indoor bender river system
a thirty two foot
North Fork simulation

where the first lab-born
benders were born
into a climate controlled
aqueous vision

> the H_2O temperature
> mimics what's up w/ the elements
> happening in real time
>
> the lights are set to reflect the levant
> to dim and illumify
> and incorporate shadows
> cast by the pineline on the shore
>
> when it rains outside
> sprinklers precipitate
>
> & as the current flows continuously
> in this totally protected
> replication of a perfect system
> a nest box is visible

it's a squat concrete under-tunnel
leading to a mating cave
w/ a port for removing
the rosary beads
of future breeds

this is where it all started
back in 2006/2007

this is where I ask
my burning question of Bendery:

"So if the scientific consensus is that there are only 590
Ozark benders being free (at last count)
and if the cryptobrancho authorities
actually foresee these species
not lasting three decades
will all this effort
really pay off?"

and the answer, of course
is as evident as the fervor
in this massive
bunker of Glurk:

"That's what we're shooting for"
Mark tells me w/ a shrug
suggesting he isn't totally certain
but they sure as hell
ain't gonna stop.

XIX. AWAITING THE NEXT EUREKA

más tanks
 muy spawn

a towering Babylon
of incubating eggs
tiered w/ aeration
to mimic the males
rocking haunches
flubbering flaps

then more more & archives more
an entire living library
of highly imperiled
bendographics

dynasties of DNA
galleries of glurkery
the most massive
impressive
collection of snot
otters on the planet

culminating in two parallel
 forty foot long
 six foot deep
 outdoor Ozark river systems
 one for North Forkers
 the other for Eleven Points

to keep the gene pools partisan
because there just might be
more subspecies than we think

I heard it from my colleague Don Shepard
Salamander Savant at U Louisiana at Monroe

& now I'm hearing it from
the Ron Goellner Center:

it's looking like thére could be
way more glurking strains
up in them thar
hillbilly hills

so stay tuned to the St. Louis Zoo
for the next major
hellbender breakthrough!

XX. MORE DISCOVERY =
MORE RESPONSIBILITY

Yep, there might be four
or even eight
genetically unique
gene pools of Ozarkians

which is more than just an epiphany
it's a satori of salamanderous significance
that will no doubt revise the science
of an entire eco-niche

more importantly
in cahoots with Arkansas Game and Fish
and the Missouri Department of Conservation
the Ron Goellner Center releases
hundreds of hellions per year

some are recaught and accounted for
but most just disappear
where they go, nobody knows

in fact, nobody knows
where the eclectic
wild child hides

what we do know though
is that 600 divided by four
or six 600 divided by eight
means a whole lot more
of a whole lot less
true chromosomal homes

because if you cross
the Current w/ the White
or Eleven Points w/ other sources
of hellbending habitat
then you homogenize
specific genetics

potentially
that's what we're looking at
more exact helixes
to study and protect
so therefore more
genomics to stock

                    meaning more urgent work to do
                    as even more species go to hell
                    in a glurking handbasket.

XXI. HENCE IN HELLBENDIA

and in Allegheny specifically
there are hatcheries where glurkers glom
glumming up to nine inches long
and are then released
as refugees

radio-tags have been implanted
to track the Easterns through the Glurk
only to find that four to eight
percent continue
to survive

"Best Management Practices" however
have been developed for the lumber industry
addressing construction of logging docks
unpaved roads
skid trails
& fire breaks

        still
        these BMPs are just "suggested"

        but outreach is on the rise
        some are sent to parks and zoos
        even Indian reservations
        for research & education

the PR of Mass Bendery
also targets local schools and hunting shows
where biologists have doubled down on Glurkitude

additionally
signs have been placed in the public eye
telling recreationists
to leave the under-rocks alone
and to let harmless
hellbenders be

                 which has actually led to fishermen
                 releasing and reporting them
                         rather than smashing
                         their glurking heads

                 —which used to be the norm.

XXII. KEEPING IT REAL

Indiana is currently
establishing baseline conditions
for awareness and perceptions
of the benders in their midst
and data from these efforts
is now being analyzed
to evaluate effectiveness

helpthehellbender.org
was launched back in 2012
this "clearinghouse for hellbender info"
lists actions locals can take

in the meantime
educators can request
classroom presentations
plus posters and stickers
for the kids

      —as Purdue U offers
      electronic field trips
      focused on genetics
      which reach over 4000 studii per year
      from 350 schools
      spanning 28 states

      —as publicity teams collaborate
      w/ community colleges from other states

      —as a mascot named Herbie the Hellbender
      shows up at civic events
      handing out bobbers touting the slogan
          "HELP THE HELLBENDER
          CUT THE LINE"

XXIII. SPEAKING OF FISHING

(the unfounded fear of coming in contact
w/ the slick of bender slime
goes back to a bunk mythology
from an old time Seneca saying
that "hellbenders got
the devil in them")

((the mucous released w/ adrenaline
can indeed be lethal to white mice
but for paws and claws
it's more of a gooey
gluey substance
that deters because
it's hard to rub off))

[hellbender slime
has also been rumored
to be shockingly electric
but that's just more
bogusness]

{of course
there's a universal paranoia
among misinformed adamant anglers
that pretty much all bottom feeders
w/ a face that only a mother could love
are out to devour
mucho gamefish populations
starting with their nests}

//but as of yet
no roe has been discovered
in any hell-eesophagi//

<<as for leaving a hook
in intestines
highly acidic stomach acids
dissolve steel
in due time>>

.

XXIV. EMPIRE & INDEPENDENCE

New York is currently developing
a smartphone app
to report benders
helling in their habitats

     NY also has a mascot costume
     housed at the Buffalo Zoo
     to spread the Gospel of the Glurk

        local tribes
        are now raising benders
        as are zoos in the Bronx and Rochester
        to supplement the Appalachian
        populations
        trying to get by

Pennsylvania
on the other hand
has produced the first
     student run
     public school
     research facility
for amphibians
in the world

     the Clarion Limestone Research Center
     studies the crashes & crises
        affecting Salamundio

        they also have an artificial river system
        waiting for inhabitants
        from the Crypto
        Glurkisphere.

XXV. PIMP MY HELLBENDER:
A LESSON IN SUSTAINABILITY

North Carolina's
Wildlife Resources Commission and
the NC Zoological Park
have teamed up to assess
hellbender status and habitat

they speak w/ anglers and landowners
gain river access and conduct surveys
on the importance of benders as bio-indicators
and they frame these discussions
in terms of both
glurkers & trout

Rocky the actual hellbender
appears at regular festival gigs
where hell-face-paintings take place
enviro info is handed out
and ambassadors of Glurkery
speak proudly & publicly

               while Snotty the Snot Otter
                   (another mascot)
               strolls amidst the masses
               generating buzz

       & over at the Zoo
       the gift shop sells
            hellbender shirts
            hellbender buttons
            and decals to promote
            hellbender consciousness
            by providing a makeover

ie, posters proclaiming
"UGLY'S ONLY SKIN DEEP"
in which cartoon glurkers
pose with a panda mask
and pink baby volgos
snuggle up in swaddling clothes

　　　　of course, this highly successful model
　　　　can be applied to other creatures
　　　　commonly perceived as out of grace
　　　　to strike a balance in the Wild.

XXVI. THE VOLUNTEER STATE
STEPS TO THE PLATE

the Tennessee Wildlife Resources Agency
& the Tennessee Hellbender Recovery Partnership
recently won a prestigious
State Wildlife Action Award
in excellence in leadership
      for the preservation
      of Eastern glurks

"environmental DNA"   a revolutionary
quasi-forensic   detection system
for shed genetic material   has been applied
to pinpoint populations

    a new cryopreservation technique
    employs the first ever
    Gene Bank of Amphibia
    w/ hormonal induction
    to artificially
    fertilizate

raging Ranaviruses   are also being studied
and there's a fifty foot   bio-bayou
at the Chattanoogazoo   to copy what
St. Louis   do do
    (captive-breeding-wise)

    Lee U has teamed up   with the Nashville Zoo
    Middle Tennessee U   Project Orianne
    San Francisco State   & an Aussie Antwerpian
    in order to collaborate on hellbendy
      initiatives

meanwhile the T   WRA
has launched an eReg   awareness campaign
to inform & destigmatize   while encouraging
quick release

       the big news though   is from 2012
       when the Nville Zoo   bred the first
       captive Easterns   in existence

      but where   O Nashville
is yr country western ballad   of the benders birthed
                   in Tennessee?

XXVII. DOORS TO A JUSTITIA-OMNIBUS-OLD-DOMINION-BUCKEYE-STYLE BENDERPALOOZA OF PC PR

• DC's Hellbender Brewery
> hosts a "Suds n' Salamanders" event
at the Smithsonian National Zoo
> where the Haunted Salamander Lab
allows visitors to observe
> glurkers glurking in the night

    • the VA Dept. of Game and Inland Fisheries
> has developed a field-based program
> for hellbender publicity
> in which 400 annual children
>> learn about crypto-physio-
>> ecology

    while a plastic hellbender statue
>> tours the world
> spreading "Hellbender Fever"
> wherever it goes

• Ohio's brainchild
> the "IF YOU SEE THIS SALAMANDER,
> LET US KNOW" business card
> is making the rounds to fishermen
>> surveyed in the field

>> live exhibits of hardy hellbenders
are featured at the Columbus and Toledo zoos
>> w/ info on dilemmatry

& property owners are now witness
to transmitter implant surgeries
in their own front yards;
the photographs they take
spark stories and memories
especially w/ kids

so to plagiarize (and improve)
on the lyrics of Jim Morrison:

"hellbenders bleeding
on dawn's early highway
crowd the child's
eggshell mind."

XXVIII. BUT BACK TO OZARKIA

where the Ozark Hellbender Working Group
initiates studies and cooperates on field work
    w/ researchers from
    federal and state agencies
    zoos and the academy
    nonprofit orgs
    and random eco
    individs

thereby developing
a propagation protocol
through watershed
protectification

    populations are monitored for fitness
    captive "head-starters" are raised for release
    local law enforce and landowners
    watch for suspicious activities
    as specialists test
    for hell-sperm quality
    metal levels
    eggcetera

    the University of Missouri—Rolla
    has been evaluating system strength
    hormones and contaminants
    thru hematology & serum work

    plus U-Mizzou is in collab
    w/ the MO DNR
    studying movement and survival patterns

there's also an outline for the recovery
of Ozark Hellbendiness
promoting "near-term recovery actions"
while providing "range-wide conservation context"
for the US Fish & Wildlife Service

Jeff Briggler *et al.*
wrote the *Hellbender Conservation Strategy* (2010)
the Bible of Hellbendery
for a super powered partnership

    of the AGFC, the MDC
    the ADEQ, the NPS
    the USFWS
    and, of course
    the SLZ

(see Section XVI)

      would you like some fries with that?

XXIX. BENDERMANIA DISCLAIMIA

and yea this sort of active interest   is taking place
all across Amerigo

hellbender distribution   is being tracked
in West Virginia, South Carolina   Kentucky, Mississippi
and Alabama databases

the Columbus Zoo
is currently working   with eDNA
while West Virginia   and Maryland
test habitat   augmentation
reintroduction   and bender rearing
from wild eggs

video borescopes   to document nesting sites
are happening in O-hio   where water samples are
being filtered   for genetic traces
as they are in KY streams   where riparian habitats
are being preserved

trapping has been tried   in Alabama
survey samples are underway
and a correlation has been found
between bender abundance
and land use patterns in GA

where population trends   are under study
& buying an eagle   license plate
helps fund   hellbender conservatio

a museum-run   natural heritage program
monitors the growth & decline   of Mississippi's
glurkographics

from New England to the Ozarks   protected statuses
       have been granted

and then there are researchers   from Texas to Florida
from Arizona to Purdue   as well as the eco-media
from every place   to cyberspace
hopping on   the hell-wagon

because
    to quote eco-blogger Jenni Veal   (nooga.com)
     "North America's largest salamander
      is a rockstar within
        the scientific community"

which may or may not be true   depending on whether
you see these poster children   for extirpation
        as celebrities   or canaries

        but and
        unfortunately
        this list can't
        keep going on

               not here
               not now
               not in this
               limitedness

      where quite a few geographies
        and quite a few agencies
           invested in myriad
           bender biotics
           are being bypassed
           in this

               chance
               glance

& so
in casting this ephemeral net
it's time to stick a fork in it

    —w/ sincere regrets,
    yr hardly humble
    narrator.

XXX. LISTEN CHUCK,

what it all comes down to
is that the prospect of a warming climate
is the albatross of Hellbendage

  threat of drought & less cold currents
  are confusing insect hatching times
  which are now combining
  w/ a plethora of other factors
  to make rivers in
                  hospitable

  some studies say
  glurkers only have
  twenty years
  whereas others report
  a soaring probability
  of impending extinction
  coming to a stream near you

as Salamander Super Scientist
Dr. David B. Wake remarks   (*Salamander News,* no. 2, 2014)
  "Human population growth
  and all that flows from it,
  from basic habitat destruction
  to global climate change"
  is the biggest threat
  for benders in this century

when asked in what ways the public can assist
he replies "First and foremost,
work for human population control"
before working on habitat
preservation or restoration

but even more importantly
he adds
admit "that WE
are the problem."

BOOK III

GLURK SPECIMEN B14!

XXXI. BIRTH OF SPECIMEN B14

laid in mid winter
up an icy Ozark creek
a softball sized glob of hellbender huevos
made from two gooby tubes
of marble sized gelatin blobs
flurbilates in the undertaint
of a four pound patriarch
known to the humans of the hollow
as Old Lasagna Sides

then suddenly they larvate forth
no longer than a squiggle inch

das venter is unpigmented
& they have no visible limbs
just nubby lobes up front
though mouth and eyes
clearly defined

they essentially look
like chubby sperms
chugging around
w/ distended
yellow guts

then suddenly
SMORGASBORD!

even Old Lasagna Sides
doesn't know why
he gobbles down
his own DNA

but he does
and he vomits
and from that
gurgitation

one spawn
lights off like a hobo
w/ a sweet potato pie.

XXXII. B14 TAKES TO THE STREETS

hunkering under a mussel shard
in the chert of an eddy bed
percolating oxygen
B14 has no clue
of what the glurking
hell to do

so he just sits there
à la protein bellypack
digesting the day away

for five weeks
lengthening and growing thinner
he just huddles in that shadow
watching his more daring siblings
succumb to the suck of random chubs

after absorbing all his nutrients though
the hunger hits him in his gut
so one night he ventures out
into the current's tug
& swishes his way upstream

there's a shaded shallow to the right
where the stiller warmer waters offer
some insects and invertebrates

B14 wiggles in
gorging on the glurkery
with a trio of his littermates

within a few minutes
they're stuffed to their frilly gillage
and bulging like balloons

their gravitation is natural
as they bunch up & burrow in
chilling in the graveltude

and it's nice
to snuggle up and know
they're not alone
glurping burping
in the night.

XXXIII. B14 - B18
TRY TO KEEP LARVATING ON

at ten weeks after hatching
now almost two inches long
obsidian and half as gilled
w/ bloopy heads and padddletails
plus digits forming on their limbs
B14 and his sibs
have become much more
active swimmers

at night they motor thru the reeds
but the thing is
greenhouse gasses they can't see
are making that shallow
shallower

so they strike out
in search of a honey hole
polywogging along the shore

—when disaster strikes
in the form of a smallmouth bass
waiting in the watercress

two hellions audibly "Glurk!"
as the jaws of the predator snap
their personal survival rate
has just gone from a hundred percent
straight down to zero zed

but B14 and B15
weave deep
into the tangle
of a sprout-like labyrinth
where they cower under spongy moss
peeking out
primevally.

XXXIV. B15 BITES THE DUST

at seven months
B14 and his sister
find a swollen bullyfrog
suspended in their chillyhole

they're patrolling the bank as usual
searching for shrimpy things
but that fatty gog-eyed froggy
is just floating there
all lazy in lethargy
until its sudden lunge

B15 is snared by a tubey tongue
and B14 sees her blur
disappear w/ a sonic SMAKK
punctuating tragic fact
that she is now
totally toast

so once again
B14's a lone wolf
glurking on & glurking fast
because here comes the bloat-frog again—

glurking spastic
B14 thrusts himself
into the rapid binary roil
of two parts hydrogen
one part oxygen

which rushes him past
the source of his genesis
then many miles downstream
& into a new
alien terrain.

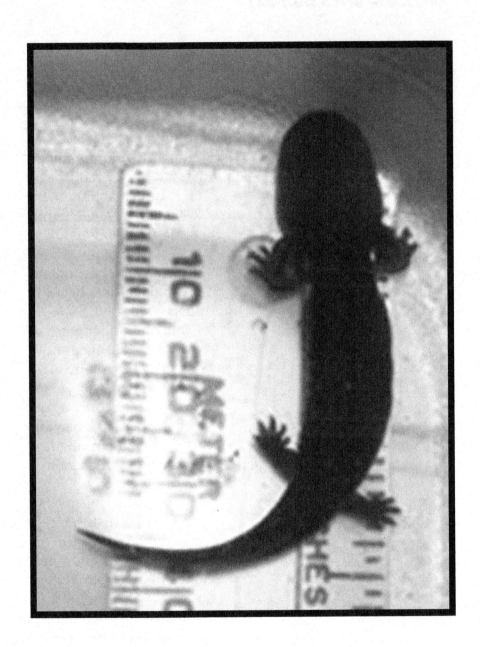

XXXV. GLURK THE GRAND NEW UNIVERSE!

the gates to this underworld
are the rusty trusses of a bridge
holding up a county road
where the artifacts of the ethersphere
glitter like a treasure trove

crushed cylinders of chromy allōy
slashy shards of transparo amorphitude
"Wal—"shreds of waving plasti-tapestries
vulcanized rings of rubber Woww
McWadded w/ papyral pulp

B14 cannot conceive
of the roll he plays on this strange stage
but he shimmies in anyway
past diaper snag & 12V battery
an amazing petro-chem sarcophagi
of garden variety pesticides
& two headless
Barbie dolls

into a sparkling new Disneyworld
a Shangri-La of shopping carts
bicycle parts
even a gaping
washing machine

and that's where he hunkers down
in the murkwomb of a rotting shoe
complete w/ soggy sock inside

and that's where
the sickness
kicks in.

XXXVI. A NEURO-PHYSIO-EXACERBATION LAMPREYS ON IN THE VOID

it's in the swirling nitrogen
compounded by the septic glurge
slurging from a trailer's anus

but B14 doesn't know
the chemistry of what
he's glucking up
through vitelline veins
& frankly ma'am
he doesn't give a damn

he's just glad to be away
from whatever it was he can't recall
that threatened his short term memory

in the meantime
his system of immunity
begins a slow and laborious
spleen spiral of acid eke

still
there's a constant buffet of drowned worms
splopping from the gutter above
& drifting past his vestibule

which makes every day for B14
Thanksgiving
in the Abyss.

XXXVII. ENTER THE DEMON PSEUDOEPHEDRIN

as B14 settles in
not needing to venture out

as B14's chronology
increases as the weeks pass by

as B14 fails to notice
a tattooed orangutan
ambling down from a single wide
and dumping in a Suda-sludge
brewed from the makings of meth

it becomes even easier
to just sink into the funk
eating at his pancreas

as a leech gloms on
and then another

as B14 just wakes and sleeps
eats and excretes

as mutagens do
what they always do
maggot-chewing
into meat.

XXXVIII. HAPPY BIRTHDAY B14

you are one year old today
just over three inches long
and yr lateral folds are beginning to form
across yr browning epiderm

you never rise to the surface
you never take a gulp of air
you just sit there like a diabetic loser
waiting for the welfare worms

but now that it's winter
they never come
so you are forced to crawl about
traversing a faux Christmas tree
a burst open garbage bag
& a bright orange oil filter
anointed w/ Valvoline

each lift of limb
sends a swarm of hornet stings
each nod of neck
crunches junctions
of vertebrae

you huff a rubber
forego a tampon applicator
& snarf an anemic snail

there are no larvae here
and there are no sparkling spawn
just globs of gum and emaciated crawdads
creeping thru dysglurkery

unto a busted mayonnaise jar
where a vibing in yr lateral line
signals a squiggle
in yr midst

something smelling like your cortex
something rising like a cobra
glurking in the toxic broth.

XXXIX. OL' NECTURUS THE FARAWAY

is the most butt ugly mudpuppy
to ever ascend from the depths of hell

but B14 holds his ground
he's willing to fight
to hold his claim
upon his Elysium

but Ol' Necturus the Faraway
has no battle in his spine
just two ancient laser eyes
blazing from the center
of a skull medusaed
by tendrils of chromo-
damaged cilia

no words pass between
B14 & the Serpentine
they just stare each other
to the quick

& in that transaction
a series of visions
leaps via ESP

because that's the way
Ol' Necturus rolls
sirening amphiumally

& hypnotized, Styxmatized
our pretty much
brancholess protagonist
gleans this un
creation myth:

XL. & LO, EIGHT THOUSAND BENDCESTORS

used to wend through these mtn streams
but then came the Great Deluge
washing almost
all away

this flood, of course
had little to do with water use
and more to do with land abuse
for the land that affected the water
infected the water
& not just metaphorically

   it was a time when oceanic acids
   were being perverted
   by a much more
   bitter Ph

   it was a time when forty percent
   of planetary phibians
   were considered "endangered"

         (www.npr.org/player/v2/
      mediaPlayer.html?action=1&t=1&islist=
       false&id=379117018&m=379381354)

it was a time when a third of sea species
were envisioned to go extinct
by the fini of the century
which caused no pause
for the Vast Blind Carbonic Pump

it was a time when the polar caps
were melting at a rate
of ten percent every decade

it was a time when
everything depends on water
as it always has

        & in this Terrible Turgid Tumble of Time
        when amphibians were labeled
        "the world's most endangered
        class of animals"

                (Terry Gross re:
            E. Kolbert's *Sixth Extinction*
                  Henry Holt, 2014)

        scientists argued
        that a catastrophic mass extinction
        for amphibians was underway

                but guess what?
                no one spoke up
                for your fore-
                fathers or mothers
                so no one
                spoke for you.

XLI. "THE AMPHIBIAN CRISIS"

so named by the nameless
took a toll on frogs 'n toads
but couldn't even make prime time

even yr skin-kin
the Panamanian golden frog
was missed by the radar
of mainstream culture

      those bright yellow symbols of good luck
      which used to range all over the place
      sunning on trees and clinging to leaves
      were wiped out in a moment's notice
                by a squalid
                    scurvy
                        fungal disease

there were herpetols however
at the Houston Zoo & other venues
who oracled a mega mycosis
so built an awesome Ark

otherwise known as the El Valle Amphibian Conservation Center
where transplanted golden frogs
now leap and gleep with harlequins
in the wilds of Central America

it's a rescue project that can only handle
one species at a time
when thousands disappear
      every year

      when the only ark for your people
      is a bunker in the bowels of a zoo

but that's not your habitat
there is no ark for that

there is only the triptych fact

that THIS IS   AN EXTINCTION CRISIS
I SAID THIS IS   AN EXTINCTION CRISIS
BECAUSE THIS IS   AN EXTINCTION CRISIS

and it's happening   on your clock.

XLII. THE JOURNEY OUT

ONTF drops the mic
and B14 is stunned dumb
by the most rousing call to arms
he has ever mentally received
from a super old
mudpuppy

although B14
can't retain a single vision
of what he just witnessed in the Amphi-Mind
every single light-sensitive cell
rippling in his wiggle-skin
knows exactly what to do

he has to take
this grail from this limbo
and make his way back
                    to the breeding scene
    then grow up as fast he can
                    to supplement his sala-strain

so he strikes out
swishilating into the churn
dingle-leeches dangling
all organs a-heave
                w/ caustic chug

                it takes over an hour
                to make it past the overpass
                when he finally takes a break
                hiccupping heart
                beating bloody
                in his breast

to paraphrase the waves of his brain
B14 knows
he has to cross this wilderness
or he is nothing
but nothing
to Everything
& his glands.

XLIII. LIFE SUCKS

I'm not as young as I used to be
is B14's primary thought
(translated, of course
into a quasi
Germanic tongue)

but then B14 amends that thought
into *No way, I'm just a kid*
so how could I be
so old so soon?

whatever the case
there are irritating parasites
all over his splotchéd skin
so he gets to work
grinding them against a rock

but those flexible little buggers
just stretch and cling elastically
as B14 grinds & grinds
until his forelimbs finally buckle
& he sinks into the sediment

—his battery acid //anti-freeze liver
sizzling w/ screening levels
surpassing EPA carco-limits
for sulfuric acid & propylene

—his system so thick w/ congealants
he can barely breathe
thru the capillary carburetors
dragging his engine down

                                    still
                  there's something better
                        about the water
          coursing around him now

                     something purer
                     something rinsing
                    not just over him
                 but through the pores
                     of his central core
                  pounding like
                        a jackhammer.

XLIV. EYE OF THE TIGER
SALAMANDER

B14's comatose state
only lasts half the night
when he breaks from it
he gets back to work
rubbing on a bloodsucker

he hamburgers his own skin
to shed this sanguine suck from him
he removes two from his lower jaw
then gets another in his mouth
which he chews in half
& swallows for its nutrients

then streaming ribbons crimsonly
he sets his sites on his infancy
and begins making
his way back

B14 goes all night
joints shrieking as he swims
so mostly he creeps
one hell-
step at a time

cringing gritting refluxing
in defiance of the shooting shards
slicing flesh w/ every flex

in spite of threat of paralysis
& the doggéd thought of
heart-halting atrophy

B14 presses on
creeping
crawling
bendily.

XLV. FUNDAMENTAL PILGRIMAGE

B14 crawls for miles
and since the solution
to pollution
is often dilution
(rinse, repeat
rinse, repeat)
he's in a lot better shape
than when he set out
weeks ago

his tendons have unstiffened
his sockets have uncalcified
as B14 treks by night
rests by day
and keeps on glurking on
always avoiding
his own kind

he'll get to that later
that's what he figures
driving on relentlessly
not even recalling
why he's compelled
to keep on trucking

the apparition of Ol' Necturus
is encoded in his DNA
meaning this achieved behavior
has revised his ascribed

which he follows w/ the fervor
of a suicide bomber
striving for a martyrdom.

XLVI. RETURN TO ICHYTHA

then free of leeches & cut w/ sinew
all six packed and ribbed w/ snap
he arrives at the abandoned
slab of his birth

B14 just knows it is
B14 moves on in
and when a brother
comes knocking on his mancave door
B14 runs him off   like a stray w/ mange

this is his spot   this is his hole
which he made his way
through hell to claim

so when a pesky goggle eye
gets up in his grille
B14   launch lurches
into the fray
clawing thrashing
gnashing away

he even smites a sister away
because this is his turf, buster
and anyone who questions
his dominion here
will face the apotheosis
of his wrath

yep, that's the way
B14 has become
and if you've got a problem w/ that
then you can kiss
his glurking butt!

XLVII. B14 HEADS OUT FOR FASTFOOD

the second summer after hatching
the gills of B14 recede
he is now four inches long
& patrolling along
on his nightly
thirty yard creep

till a single *ZINGLE*
zizzles in his ripple-tissue
as he senses a stench
so fetid in putritude
that he can hardly navigate
so swoops ahead
to rubberneck

it's a dead chub
fringed w/ gauzy rot
but even better than that
there's a terra cotta crayfish
chowing down in necro-town

it's almost as long as B14
who instinctively knows
what his mighty maw can do

employing a highly unusual
mode of asymmetrical suction feeding
his bilateral mandibles
erupt like an aimed net

and as this happens
(envision in slow mo)
his throat expands, ballooning out
as his prey is drawn in w/ a jet

to a highly flexible pair of jaws
where a single sweep of bottom teeth
and two concentric rows up top
clamp down w/ dragon force

two pebbles are also sucked up
along w/ some dolomite dust
but the crustacean is now
a calorie count.

XLVIII. THE NEW SEX SYMBOL ON THE BLOCK

by B14's third winter
aka his second year
he is 4.8 inches long
and still holding on

lacking gular folds
and visible somites
black spots gaining prominence
his horizontal skirty wings
are becoming meta
merically notched

as he sits in wait
of what's to come
digesting
defending
hunting
haunting
his run like a ghost
trapped between two worlds

because B14
the most well traveled bender
to ever traverse this stream
is still
sexually
immature

the hot young glurkies though
have their winky eyes on him
he's strong he's swift
& having recovered
from his abysmal
experience
B14
has tight genes

so they giggle and wiggle from a distance
which he can sense just as much
as the pulsating groaning
in his
groinflashery.

XLIX. A QUANTUM LEAP
THRU ADOLESCENCE

all solid and meaty and muscular
having survived his sixth winter
studly Specimen B14
now a foot long
finally dares to tread upstream
farther than he's ever
glurked before

for some reason
he just takes off

he passes his cove of larvitude
glimmers a vision
of snuggling in puppitude
then shakes his head in fuddlement
continuing on

five more nights crawling on
five more days hunkering down
as the streamlining stream
narrows w/ force

he only goes a country mile
but to B14
these uncharted hinterlands
are as foreign as the moon

shimmering the way ahead
beaconing him
to a roaring rush

of a smashing crashing cataract
grinding shells to dust.

L. BEWARE THE PORTALS OF THE UNKOWN

the trip has been rough
w/ little food in the last expanse
and from the acrid musk
B14 is snuffing up
he has an idea why

meanwhile
the water is high
so the falls are low
in this drought
stricken
stretch

so pushing on & pushing in
B14 braves the crush
torquing twisting bendering up
and makes it to the other side

where an unforeseen tranquil pool
is packed w/ mollusks & gastropods
and the buffet is free
and open to the public

or so he believes
after stuffing gut
then searching for
a hidey hole

there's a log ahead
jammed beneath the river roots
of an oak/hickory entanglement
w/ a preordained opening
conveniently facing
downstream

calling
so it seems
for B14
to waltz on in.

LI. LUKE, I AM YOUR FATHER
(ALLEGHENY-ALLIGATOR-STYLE)

& when he does
he's not alone
there's something in there next to him
something familiar
yet alien

it's the source of that bitter stank
smoking chodely from some glands
which B14 can't see
w/ feeble eyes

nevertheless
B14 gets a feel
for the crypto creature
just inches from his patty-head

it's Old Lasagna Sides
sucking up his own sloughed skin
& staring back
w/ glurking smirk

the father strikes
like lightning in the blacknight hole
and B14 is in the grip
of an angry alpha
twice his size

they grapple   they grabble
& B14 is twisted around
then all of a sudden
going down

throaty acids wash around
his gill-less slits
as the elder snorts and horks
hoovering
his legacy.

LII. TO THE POINT THAT B14

in the gorge of Old Lasagna Sides
has to give it up
there's nothing he can do
but await the final
fatal glurk

But wait! what's that?

a fandangly strang of inner skin
hanging like a scrotal sack

it's a uvula
and B14 chomps on
holds on
& spins

"GLAAARP!!"
Old Lasagna Sides
rupes him up

and B14
shoots for the river's skin
erupts over the waterfall
and flounders down the other side

where he scampers like no glurking glurker
has ever glurking glurked before
swaying like a racing snake
all the way back to his home base

where huddling under slabitude
& burning w/ raw frazzlement
Specimen B14
vows in his own hellbender way
to never stray that way again

it's a promise he will always keep
even when the reason
ingrained in his brain
becomes a phantom
phibian thought.

LIII. THE SEASONS CYCLE CYCLICALLY

and B14
takes a mate
then another
passing on
deoxy strands

he will later see
the larvae of his loins
but never feel the yearn
to swallow purge
their selfiness

he's achieved what he set out to do
even though he can't remember
his impetus to infiltrate
this tributary w/ his spawn

when suddenly
he is startled into the light
some air ape above
has jacked his casa

they've been here before
they've kidnapped kin
& clipped their toes
as a primitive form
of mark-recap

a rubbery hand reaches down
grabs B14 like a burrito
and causes him
to secrete

a thick sticky goo
which is annoying to channel cats
but hardly as venomous
as old wives
perpetrate.

LIV. ON THE LAM AGAIN

it's a gluey substance
and it's hard to rub off
but it doesn't deter
the abductor above

so B14
reverts to his next defense
his jaws snap trigger clamp
penetrating polydermis

"YIIIIIII!" guy cries
this 'stonished student of the Glurk
tossing B14 into the drink

where hellbending hellaciously
power propelling his way downstream
B14 escapes the threat
of possible PIT
telem inject

or lab life under light
of hormone induced
experiment angst

you never know what these creatures will do
why once in 1967
E.D. Robin removed a lung
to see if Tweegs could get along
w/out this vestigial apparatus

(incidentally
that glurker glurked on
thereby proving
such organs are for buoyancy)

& another time
back in 1824
R. Harlan sent a bender straight to hell
by placing it in brackish water

Specimen B14 however
never knew those hellatives
or their hell-narratives

all he knows
is that bros have been bashed upon the rocks
and that sisters have been hauled up by their guts

which is why
all frantic and freaking out
he winds his way downstream
all the way past
a familiar Abyss

& into a strange new hydro flow
coming from a fracking ditch

and I tell you this:

there is no sequel for B14
only the chaos of eviscerating skin
disemboweling from within
and the stranglehold
of asphyxia

meaning
life becomes
a bummer extreme
for our hero
B14.

BOOK IV

AFTER THE OZARKIANS

LV

But seriously, folks
let's get back to the facts
and the fieldwork...

Knowing that US Fish & Wildlife
and Arkansas Game and Fish
were spending a week hellbendering
in the NE corner of the state
I shot on up to Pocahontas
& found their trailered trucks

then burst into Larry's Pizza
like an invasive species

herpetologist Kelly Irwin (AGFC)
was having dinner
and was not amused
he said he'd call but I came up
because, as I stressed
"I just gotta get in
on this research!"

a big bald muscled man
Kelly sighed and let me in
but not w/out the understanding
that he's the Captain
and if I intend to take up space on his boat
he's sure as hell gonna put me to work

"Aye aye," I replied
and shook hands w/ the crew
salamanderous veteran Chris Davidson (USFW)
Tennessee State grad candidate Jeronimo Silva from Brazil
and a gar-flash from the past
Tommy Inebnit w/ the Feds
all of them bound
by Crypto-Brancho
Glurkery.

LVI

"Ask me anything!"
Captain K commanded me
stuffing face
     w/ mediocre pizza

so I started with the St. Louis question
whether the WildCare was working
and he replied an emphatic YES

and he should know
having spent fifteen years
leading the Ozark Bender Brigade
with Jeff Briggler out of MO

who, with his staff
developed the hellbender huts
and leads the charge to repopulate
the compromised systems

which the St. Louis Zoo
has been supplementing
with hundreds of benders
every year

"At a time when these species"
     I prodded
"are facing multiple challenges…"

Capt. K just shook his head
"In addition to chytrid fungus"
he told me
"there's a new flesh-eating bacteria now"

to paraphrase
Captain K then told me
how practically all Ozark cryptobranchoids
are not only experiencing habitat loss
but they're infected by a type
of toxic yuck
so they pretty much all
have crippled paws:

lesions, scars, irritated tissue
bone nubs jutting up
from jellied rot

"And," I threw in, "all at a time
when we're identifying new subspecies…"

"Independent species"
Capt. K corrected me
"each with their own
specific genetics."

LVII

Out on the Eleven Point
the following morning
ancient rounded rusting cars
trussing back the lush brush

we shoot down rapids in two
flatbottomed fiberglass boats
with jet-drive propulsion
not props

Chris and Tommy
are on the USFW craft
w/ Jason Phillips
just up from Augusta
and I'm with Capt. K and Jeronimo
in the AGFC boat

in the last two days
they've sampled five "animals"
as Captain K refers to them
but only one with
"perfect toes"

the idea is to check and place
hellbender huts
or "artificial nest boxes"
as they're commonly called

the benders enter
through a PVC penis
then tunnel into
the concrete cave
of the nuts

and then biologists come along
and do what biologists do

most boxes though
tend to be empty.

LVIII

We stop to scoop sand
into a plastic bin
then continue down
the waterway

Captain K pointing out
a series of jetties;
a stream team
built these bouldered barriers
from which sycamores
are already sprouting
the anchoring web
of their roots
keeping the sedimentation down

because benders
like bluegills
require gravel
to reproduce

it might be a losing battle though
when some land owners don't understand
that the roads they create
and the yards they scape
all along the rivershore
silt the system
totally up

the crew describes
such scenes to me
at various points
along this stretch

Capt. K adds
that when they set these boxes up
it's "like stealing from Peter
to give to Paul"

basically
you gotta go down there
and find the type of slab
a hellbender would employ
which you somehow use
to buttress a hut

but that's how it's done
gradual and slow
two steps forward
          (hopefully)
for every one
we take back.

LIX

down down the river we go
the electric blue August sky
a bald eagle
     skimming by
  a juvenile coon
      swimming to the other shore
  plus club-tailed dragonflies
   & drymud softshells
      slipping in

to Vern's Hole
where Captain K explains
the two main purposes
of the huts:

1) to supplement habitat
& 2) to find nesting activity
for eggs to headstart

"In 2001," Capt. K says
"this site yielded fourteen animals
that's the most we've ever had
from one spot"

    go figure.

LX

As Capt. K and Jeronimo
suit up to dive
I ask how the chytrid
is affecting other amphibians

Captain K tells me
it's mainly through messing
with reproduction; that is
it screws up organs internally
throwing a wrench
into the process

"Take the wood frog,"
Capt. K adds as an example
then goes into a vivid description
of horrified biologists
witnessing a mass die off

"But what about other salamanders?"
        I inquire
"Are they experiencing deformities
like the hellbenders?"

"Nope," the Captain states
matter of factly

Point being:
benders are now the posterboys
for an all consuming
                mutilating
                        chemical scourge

that spreads its toxic slaughter
in various forms   in various ways
with various symptoms
manifesting differently
depending on the species
so it's not the same
every time

                            but then again
                            neither is AIDS.

Jeronimo Silva (Tennessee State U)
and Kelly Irwin (AGFC).

LXI

Captain K also mentions
the chicken house facilities
currently being
installed in the region
five to six hundred
to be unexact
and a percentage, of course
puking straight
into the Eleven Point

having just seen
a big reeking poultry plant
spewing blood 'n gunk
'n feathers plus
assorted antibiotics
into a system

I knew this vision
all too well
and how it can change
water quality
over night

but even if such defecation
isn't direct desecration
there are other pollutants
to consider

"Have you ever seen how chicken litter
gets scattered on the fields?"
            Captain K asks
"It stinks to high hell
and it's full of arsenic
for killing intestinal parasites"

so when it rains
it drains
which also affects
nitrogen levels

algae blooms
oxygen's doomed
and the next thing you know
our benders are gone

or, at least
that's the implication
as Captain K and Jeronimo
heft on lead belts

then fire up the hookah…

LXII

...rig, that is
an air compressor
for pumping O_2 down to divers
multiple hoses octopusing out

meanwhile downstream
Chris and Tommy descend as well
into the blue green soup
of what used to be a clear mountain stream
though now visibility is only three feet

I watch above as they scoot around
bubbles breaching
checking huts

"No animals"
is the verdict
"sedimentation bad"

it's been a year since these nests were checked
and the tunnels are clogged with underjunk
not even a bullhead
in residence

so we drop some more
hellboxes in.

LXIII

Here's how you do it:

you go searching around
find the right spot
then haul a hut
to a flat rock

then go get some gravel
from out in the middle
lift the lid & pour it in

there's a square hole
in the bottom of the box
the idea is to pack that gravel
so no other critters
can git in

then you go get some sand from me
which I've scooped into cups
and then you spread a bed in there

then rise into the air
where the generator's steady roar
and diesel exhaust
is sedating the cells
of my brain

so I move to the bow to be upwind
but for the benders below
they have no choice
they take what they get
        filtering in
through their skin.

LXIV

And the specimen removal
procedure's like this:

you dive down with your light
block the hut-throat with a rock
then lift the lid and peer in

if there's a hell-occupant
then you gently roll it
into a pillowcase
which has been bleached to protect
benders from bugs

then you place that pillowcase
into a diving bag
and tie it to
the side of the boat

but alas there are
no hellbenders here
in the most fruitful hell-
hole on the river

so we continue downstream
passing more turtles
        sunning in the sun
passing more kingfishers
        kingfishing
passing more herons
        skronking honkily

to get to the next
hellbender site.

LXV

All day long we search and set
Jeronimo and Capt. K
submarining in the current
while I lug huts
to the point that I rip
my pants up the butt

and all the while
I'm looking for fish
because that's what I do

I see a few sunnies
and some minnows too
glimpse some darters
and a crayfish or two

but as for anything longer
than six inches
I don't see squat
      not even
      one
      jump

      which is a sign
      so stay tuned
      to find out why.

LXVI

Jeronimo has this t-shirt
which asks "GOT MILT?" on the front
and depicts two benders on the back
swirling in a spermy cloud

this design was part
of the 2015 Hellbender Symposium
at the St. Louis Zoo
an event I couldn't attend
due to horsing sturgeon in

I ask Captain K though
if there's been any recent
      breakthroughs in cryptobranchage

and he tells me there's now
a new way to sex
juveniles through hemo work
and it's harmless
and efficient
and will give us all
a more accurate vision
of the genders we engender

      Thanks, Blood!

LXVII

The US Fish & Wildlife boat
finally bags a robust male
which they can tell
from its rosy vent
so the boats converge
for "processing"

Jeronimo works it
free of its swaddlings
brings forth a wavy mass
of black & brown calico
a living, squiggling
lasagna lizard
screaming from a wide
                        red
                                Kermit mouth
                gleaming a line
                    of razor fine teeth

also noticeable
are tiny pink toes
gripping and flailing
like a baby

a human baby

which Capt. K
for some reason
dubs "Sparky."

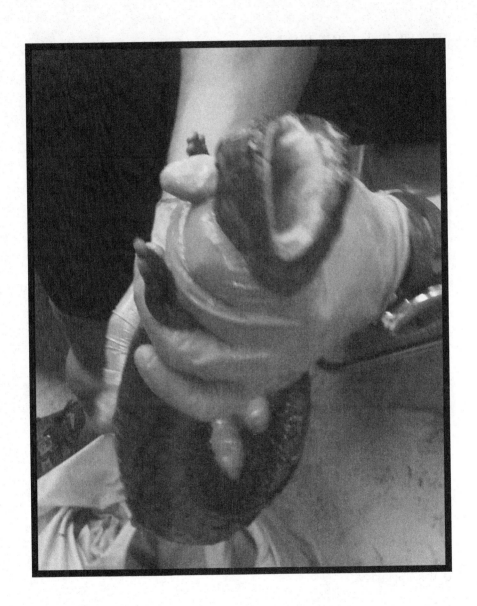

LXVIII

the Game and Fish
PIT tag scanner
is out of whack
but Captain K figures
Sparky's a "recap"

"Looks like he's been snipped before"
      he tells the crew
pointing to some spots on Sparky's swinging
oar of a tail
which he tries to use
to leverage himself
from Jeronimo's Latex grip

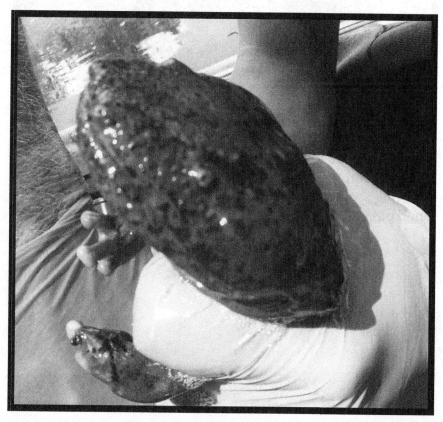

Sparky's then placed
into a Tupperware
where looking down
at gossamer streamers
ghosting white phlegm
I ask if this is the slime
that gets released
when a salamander thinks
it's a goner

a glueyness I've felt before
with mudpuppies
excreting secretions
when pierced for bait

"Yep," Captain K says, "that's the stuff.
It's a really sticky substance"

"Is it actually toxic?
        I ask

Capt. K laughs
and goes into a story
about some guy who couldn't be outdone
so when he heard some dude
dared to taste some hellbender slime
he went and licked a full grown adult
from slimy head
to slimy tail

"Then spent the next hour
spitting in the river
and washing his mouth"
          Captain K tells us

needless to say
none of us feel the burning urge
to pass Sparky around
and take a hit.

LXIX

Packing sand was easy work
so Captain K is adamant
that I assist him
in the instant

he orders me to grab a vial
and then a swab
with which he gathers goo
from between Sparky's
little piggies

Sparky Gets a Swabbing.

which he wiggles
in protest
clenching and unclenching
infantly

I then clip the stem
off the swab
seal the vial
and we put it in
the dry ice cooler

that's the test for chytrid fungus
so next comes the test
for Ranavirus!

> which has become a major
> infectious factor
> in the global decline
> of salamanders

using what looks like a cigarette
Capt. K presses its tubiness
into a spot on Sparky's tail
which I tweezer into
another vial
this one requiring
no refrigeration

the samples are now
ready for analysis.

LXX

I first noticed the orangy coloration
when we turned Sparky on his belly
to measure his amphibious length
he had a motley tangerine sheen
like rusty iron seepages
oozing on a muddy shore
and again those funny fingers
a-wigglin' at the sky

Sparky is 470 millimeters
or eighteen and a half inches long

and then we weigh him in a milk jug

Sparky is 607 grams
meaning almost 1.4 pounds

not bad for a Cryptobranchidae

who, from his constant squirmings
seems healthy enough.

LXXI

But that's the rub
because there's another rub
all over Sparky's toes

in some places
the nubs have been worn
past the bone

none of us really saw this at first
but then we took inventory

on one front paw
Sparky is missing a thumb
and not only that
there's a leech attached

on the other hand
he's pretty much missing
everything

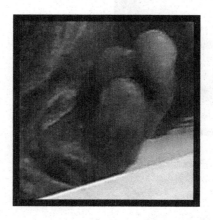

"You see how his toes are bulbous like that?"
      Captain K says
"That's scar tissue building up
those toes should be tapered
like on the back feet"

which are a bit inflamed
but not so much the mangled meat
as the stumpy stubs
Sparky employs
to pull himself
across the rocks
            every.
                  single.
                        hellbending.
                              day.

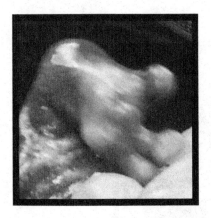

LXXII

I can hardly stare
at Sparky's screwed up phalanxes
which, in effect
make him human
or about as human
as a creature can be

whether we acknowledge it or not
we look for ourselves in animals
we personify eyes and appreciate
bipedal activity

monkeyfaces are always pleasing
and whatever species we extrapolate
into visions of ourselves
the babies are always
funner to ponder

that's why we like silly photos
of puppies driving toy cars
or Grumpy Cat memes
exuding human crankiness

so if there's one thing about the bender
that endears them to us
it's their wigglific paws

because when you stare a bender in the eye
you end up focusing
on its toes

which, in essence
is our connection
with this aspect
of the Wild.

LXXIII

Toes of Amphibious Evolution Undulating Infernally!

Toes of Tectonics Making for Mass Mountains and
Crystalline Streams!

Toes of Mucho Ameri-Cultures and All Their Gone
Hellbendy Lore!

Toes of Sustenance, Witchcraft, & Scaring Away Mother-In-
Laws!

Toes of Rumors of Barking Benders Launching Full On
Rabid Attacks!

Toes of an Annual Celebration Embodied in a Statuesque
Grotesque Salamanding in the Street!

Toes Those Links in a Food Chain Ranging from Teeny
Weeny Micro-Organics Right on up to Us!

Toes of Asian Cryptozillas Stumbling from the Underworld
in the YouTube Blaze of Day!

Toes of Being Preyed upon More than They're Prayed upon!

Toes of Ovipositing Ribbons of Glorious Glutinous Goo!

Toes of the Hellbender Dance, Rocking in Nest for Two or
Three Months!

Toes of Our Bio-Barometer and the Acid Rain Is Still Coming
Down!

Toes of a Nonrefundable Natural Diversity Swirling into the
Septic Stew!

Toes of Chytrid Fungus, Ranavirus, and Myriad Other
Leprosies!

TOES CORRODING

GRODILY!!!

LXXIV

Later in my motel room
at the Rock 'n Roll Hwy Inn
(wifi password: Elvislives)
I ask myself
        what I've learned

and the first answer is obvious:
there's a consistent intensity
that's needed to keep
such projects afloat

        I saw this firsthand
        in the man hours & equipment expended
        in the data taking and diving and joking
        around with each other
        because you have to have a sense of humor
        or else you're just
        selling furniture

not to disparage that
but there's something deeper
in the depths of the Eleven Point
that might even be
a twelfth point

        it's something Captain
        K said to me
        tillering back:

        "As the hellbenders go
        so go the fisheries"

to which I'd add the caveat

"and as the fisheries go
so goes the world"

—because that's the way the crypto crumbles
as P. Floyd asserts in magnum opus
How can you have any pudding
if you don't eat your meat?

and as I didactically postulate
How can we continue to sustain
a strong and safe environment
if we allow our canaries
to waste away?

LXXV

comic relief:

Why was the hellbender invited to the party?

So they could use his head

for bean dip.

LXXVI

Let's not forget that we're in the midst of a mass extinction
our sixth mass extinction
to be exact

extinction usually occurs
at a natural "background rate"   (Center for Bio Diversity)
of one to five species per year
but now we're losing fauna at
a thousand to ten thousand times that

but for amphibians
"the planet's most threatened class of organism"
the background extinction rate
for this frontline species
        (followed by the frogs?
        followed by the toads?
        followed by the fish?)
used to be about
a species every thousand years

now   however
we're talking numbers
forty five thousand times
greater than that   (Elizabeth Kolbert's
                                                  Sixth Extinction)

some estimates estimate
two hundred to two thousand
species disappear
every year   (WWF)

others suggest
that up to a hundred and fifty
bite the dust per day   (BBC)

    all this at a time
    when thirty to fifty percent
    of planetary animals
    are projected to vanish
    by mid century   (Center for Bio Diversity)

      so here's the question:

          Where does that leave the hellbender?
          during this Rana-Chytrid-Viral plague
          of habitat loss?

      and here's the answer:

              Right at the front
              of the first frontline!

LXXVII

Like I noted before
there aren't a lot of fish in this stream
and like Captain K implied
(in agreement with the literature)
hellbenders are an indicator
of a system's overall health

more importantly though
how can we in good consciousness
not strive like we're striving?

    with hellbender huts and public outreach
    with programs for kids and ramparting plans
    with research and testing and H_2O vigilance
    with everything we need to do

how can we not   do that?
like we're not   doing for millions
             of other species?

    Meaning   ultimately
    there are more questions than answers
    when it comes to hellbenders
        those eternally damned
    tortured souls
        twisting purgatorally

                 like us
          in a way
             trying to make sense
     of a mess we never made
                 but nevertheless
            find ourselves
                  responsible for

like our skin
like their skin
like all our communal skins
subject to the Toxic Gnaw.

LXXVIII

As ridiculous as it may sound
hellbenders are our brothers
and our sisters

they're even our friends
and mothers and fathers
not to mention
next door neighbors

or babies
or Jesus
who also
allegedly
died for our sins

so let's take it from Darwin
who envisioned an amphibious missing link
crawling from the muck
to become us

there's a connection between
salamanders and sapiens
that goes way beyond
flesh dripping toes
& myriad myths

there's a connection biological
a connection purely fanciful
a connection primordial
which we will never understand
but will always be
umbilicalled to

as glurkers glurk
glurking on

glurking in murk
glurking in lurk

of what we all
glurking
Glurk.

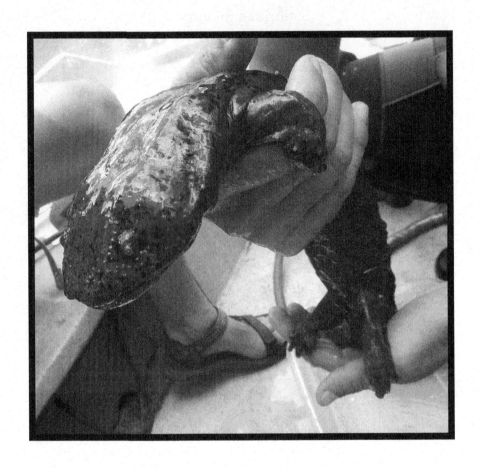

Sparky the Snot Otter
Cryptobranchus alleganiensis bishopi
Age: 15 to 30 Years Old
Released Back to the Eleven Point River
in Northeastern Arkansas
August 12, 2015.

OTHER ANAPHORA LITERARY PRESS TITLES

Film Theory and Modern Art
Editor: Anna Faktorovich

Interview with Larry Niven
Editor: Anna Faktorovich

Dragonflies in the Cowburbs
Donelle Dreese

Domestic Subversive
Roberta Salper

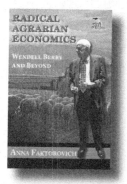

Radical Agrarian Economics
Anna Faktorovich

Fajitas and Beer Convention
Roger Rodriguez

Spirit of Tabasco
Richard Diedrichs

Skating in Concord
Jean LeBlanc

CPSIA information can be obtained
at www.ICGtesting.com
Printed in the USA
BVOW03s0756161217
502955BV00001B/85/P